Meet Marcion

Sebastian Moll

Meet Marcion

**Bibliographical Information of the
Deutsche Nationalbibliothek**
This publication is listed in the Deutsche Nationalbibliographie of the
Deutsche Nationalbibliothek; detailed bibliographical information
can be accessed under http: //dnb.d-nb.de

© 2014 Sebastian Moll
Printing, Production and Layout: BoD – Books on Demand
ISBN: 978-3-7386-6321-1

To John Armes, Michael Fuller, Marty Lunde,
Steve Martz, Paul Parvis, Sara Parvis
– The Original Ensemble

Preface

It gives me great pleasure finally to publish this play, almost ten years after its premiere in Edinburgh on November 30, 2005. Ever since, the play has been performed several times, including the unforgettable performance at Christ Church, Oxford, during the XV International Conference on Patristics Studies 2007.

Many passages in the play, particularly in the footnotes, are outdated from an academic point of view. In fact, several statements provided here are refuted by my own work "The Arch-Heretic Marcion", published in 2010. However, I have decided to present the play unchanged, considering it rather a piece of art than a research study in constant need of revision.

Bingen am Rhein, October 2014

Sebastian Moll

Es ist eine Freude, sich mit einem tief religiösen Mann von intellektueller Reinlichkeit zu beschäftigen.

Adolf von Harnack about Marcion

DRAMATIS PERSONAE

MARCION, *theologian and church leader in Rome, considered a heretic*

APELLES, *one of his followers*

TERTULLIAN, *Marcion's most ardent adversary*

PTOLEMAEUS, *Gnostic leader in Rome*

ANICETUS, *Bishop of Rome*

POLYCARP, *Bishop of Smyrna*

Scene: Rome, middle of the second century

Prologue

PLAYWRIGHT   O, for a muse of fire, that would ascend
The brightest heaven of invention,
A kingdom for a stage, princes to act,
And monarchs to behold the swelling scene!
...

Enter Theologian.

THEOLOGIAN (*interrupting him*) Stop this nonsense!
PLAYWRIGHT   You spoiled my entrance!
THEOLOGIAN And about time too! We have some serious business to attend to!
PLAYWRIGHT   Ernst ist das Leben, heiter die Kunst.
THEOLOGIAN What?
PLAYWRIGHT   Schiller said so. It means: life is serious, art is joyful.
THEOLOGIAN I'm a theologian, I know German!
PLAYWRIGHT   Maybe you understand the words, but you certainly do not understand the message. This is a work of art we are dealing with here. We are trying to paint a portrait of Marcion.
THEOLOGIAN Indeed we are. And I am here to ensure the theological and historical correctness of this enterprise.
PLAYWRIGHT   And I'm here to make sure that this will be more than just another boring lecture.
THEOLOGIAN Here we go. I said from the beginning that this project is rubbish.
PLAYWRIGHT   A wonderful attitude!

THEOLOGIAN Come on, the whole concept is a-historical from start to finish. You know that Tertullian never could have met Marcion. He had just been born when Marcion died.

PLAYWRIGHT Montesquieu was born more than 150 years after Machiavelli died, but Maurice Joly still let them meet in his *Dialogue aux enfers*. Not as a falsification of history, but in order to compare their views.

THEOLOGIAN Lousy French know-it-alls! I stick to historical facts.

PLAYWRIGHT L'essentiel est invisible pour les yeux.

THEOLOGIAN Will you stop that!

PLAYWRIGHT Well, if you prefer someone of your own kind, the great Anselm of Canterbury himself stated that those matters which are studied in the style of question and answer are more intelligible and therefore more pleasing to many minds – (*slightly sneering*) especially to those who are slower to apprehend.

THEOLOGIAN So he said indeed. But he created a dialogue with his disciple Boso, not with Augustine or someone else who lived a long time before him.

PLAYWRIGHT Are these few years between Marcion and Tertullian really such an obstacle?

THEOLOGIAN A few years? Do you realize how much happened in them? How are the two supposed to have a conversation given their completely different contexts?

PLAYWRIGHT The play will focus on Marcion. Therefore it is set in his time, in the middle of the second century. We will just have to shift Tertullian's birth about 50 years into the past.

THEOLOGIAN	So he would be in his forties then. But Marcion would already be close to his death.
PLAYWRIGHT	Well, I think we should make him a little younger too.
THEOLOGIAN	Why is that?
PLAYWRIGHT	Because I don't want to make their discussion look like one between father and son. Although we would have a nice finale then with Marcion saying to Tertullian: (*in a Darth Vader voice*) I am your father!
THEOLOGIAN	Marcion practised celibacy, you should know that!
PLAYWRIGHT	And after the performance the whole audience will know! Isn't that what your business is supposed to be about, teaching people these things?
THEOLOGIAN	Indeed, but teaching requires absolute precision.
PLAYWRIGHT	Oh yes, precision most sublime! My friend, the spirit of an earlier time, To us it is a seven-sealed mystery; And what you learned gentlemen would call Its spirit, is its image, that is all, Reflected in your own mind's history.
THEOLOGIAN	Be that as it may, you still haven't told me how you intend to turn Tertullian with all of his contextual views into a man of the second century.
PLAYWRIGHT	I believe I have a solution for that.
THEOLOGIAN	(*almost resigned*) No doubt.
PLAYWRIGHT	There are certain ideas which would definitely be anachronistic, and using them in the play would distort the historic situation I'm trying to portray. For example Tertullian's

idea of the Church, which was far more developed in his time than it was in the middle of the second century.

THEOLOGIAN Let's hope there are no Catholics in the audience.

PLAYWRIGHT On the other hand there are things which may not be as problematic as they appear at first sight. The rule of faith, for instance.

THEOLOGIAN What are you talking about? The first certain reference to the rule of faith can be found in Irenaeus.

PLAYWRIGHT The first certain reference maybe. But does that necessarily mean that the rule of faith could not have existed 30 years before?

THEOLOGIAN Well, I suppose ...

PLAYWRIGHT See, therefore our handling of Tertullian's work shall be: unless we can proof with certainty that the ideas in his work would be anachronistic in the middle of the second century, we can keep what he said. Can you live with that?

THEOLOGIAN Barely. But what about Tertullian's personal situation? Will he already have put together his complete argument against Marcion.

PLAYWRIGHT Of course not! That would be boring. I don't want their conversation to sound like "Let's talk about this topic now". I want each discussion to be born out of a particular situation, not just pieces of discourse put together. It is supposed to be a real play, not a Platonic dialogue. That is why Tertullian won't know much about Marcion when he meets him, only some rumours.

THEOLOGIAN And you really think you will be able to include all the information about Marcion in this play?

PLAYWRIGHT Well, I don't want to bore the audience for three hours, so we might not include *all* the information available. I shall therefore try to focus on topics which are still relevant and understandable for people today. And from time to time I think the audience wouldn't mind some comic relief either.

THEOLOGIAN I hope you won't forget that this is still an academic work.

PLAYWRIGHT Don't worry, every piece of conversation in this play will be based on evidence from the sources, both primary and secondary.

THEOLOGIAN What about Marcion's part? We have nothing left of what he wrote.

PLAYWRIGHT But we can conclude it from what his adversaries said about or rather against him. Our best source is of course Tertullian's work *Adversus Marcionem*.

THEOLOGIAN So Tertullian's part in the play will completely be based on his works.

PLAYWRIGHT Well, for the most part. But we should allow for some other sources as well. Tertullian for example does not provide us with much information about Marcion's life. Writers such as Irenaeus and Epiphanius are a great help in this matter, for I think the first scene should give the audience an idea of who this Marcion actually is.

THEOLOGIAN Okay. And I think the following scenes should reflect the development of Marcion's theology. We should start with what is really bothering him and move forward to those

	ideas which derive from it.
PLAYWRIGHT	See, we can work together if we try.
THEOLOGIAN	Well, I guess the plan is acceptable so far.
PLAYWRIGHT	I look forward to this fruitful cooperation.
THEOLOGIAN	(*leaving*) I warn you. No monkey business!

Exit Theologian.

PLAYWRIGHT   Admit me Chorus to this history;
Who prologue-like your humble patience pray,
Gently to hear, kindly to judge, our play.

Scene I

Something is rotten in the Church of Rome

The atrium of Marcion's villa in Rome. The decor is fairly elegant, yet modest.
Marcion is praying on his knees.
He is wearing a tunica with a thin purple stripe and a golden ring at his hand.[1]

Enter Apelles. He waits until Marcion has finished his prayer. Marcion rises, making the sign of the cross.[2]

APELLES	Brother Marcion, you have a visitor.
MARCION	What a pleasant surprise! Bring him in, brother.

Exit Apelles. He returns with Tertullian, who is wearing the pallium.[3]

APELLES	My bishop[4], this is ...
TERTULLIAN	(*interrupting him*) My name is Quintus Septimius Florens Tertullianus!

Marcion gives Apelles to understand that he may leave. Exit Apelles.

MARCION	(*warmly and with open arms*) Welcome to my home, brother. I am Marcion.

TERTULLIAN	(*disdainfully*) Is this your full name? Just Marcion?
MARCION	Marcion of Sinope, if you prefer.
TERTULLIAN	Prefer? It's getting worse and worse! So it is true that you were born in Pontus, this barbaric region far away from our more civilized waters, inhabited by strange tribes – if indeed living in a wagon can be called inhabiting. They devour their own parents' bodies at banquets, women display their naked breasts; no germ of civilization is to be found in these parts![5]
	O, how horrible it must have been for the great Ovid[6] being banned to this disgusting place without daylight, with fog instead of air, ice instead of water, where savagery is the only thing warm.[7]
MARCION	(*slightly sneering*) I see you must have been there several times yourself, my friend.[8]
	But tell me, has the great Tertullian, the magnificent jurist[9], the brilliant apologist, come all the way from Carthage to Rome, just to declare his admiration for my home country?
TERTULLIAN	I have come to investigate.
MARCION	Investigate? What exactly?
TERTULLIAN	There are rumours, Marcion, rumours about you and your new doctrine.
MARCION	I see my reputation precedes me.
TERTULLIAN	The reputation of a heretic!
MARCION	A heretic? What do you mean?
TERTULLIAN	What do I mean?! You of all people should know. Did not your own father, the most worthy bishop of Sinope, excommunicate you?[10]
MARCION	We did differ on certain issues, yes.

TERTULLIAN	You differed on whether it was right for you to seduce a virgin[11], you mean?
MARCION	That's an infamous lie! I never did such a thing! It was doctrinal differences which made me leave my home town and set for the province of Asia.[12]
TERTULLIAN	Making propaganda for your heresy, I presume.
MARCION	I did try to lead them into clarity, indeed. I had even brought some letters of recommendation from my Pontic brothers with me.[13] But ...
TERTULLIAN	But they rejected you as well[14], I understand. Wise men they are, the people of Ephesus and Smyrna.
MARCION	And so I came here.[15]
TERTULLIAN	Some say you were so scared to come to Rome that you even had to send a woman beforehand?[16]
MARCION	And some say Carthaginians are smart enough not to believe everything they hear.
TERTULLIAN	But it is true that the Roman community, after some back and forth[17], finally rejected you, isn't it? Well, all good things come in threes, as they say.
MARCION	It was a sad day to be sure, the ides of July 144[18], when the ecclesia of Rome finally decided not to accept me. Well, at least I got my 200.000 sesterces back.[19]
TERTULLIAN	200.000 sesterces?!
MARCION	Just a small welcoming present I gave them.
TERTULLIAN	Money from your pirate ships[20], no doubt.
MARCION	I am an honest merchant, brother. However, overseas trade is fairly profitable, especially

	these days.[21]
TERTULLIAN	So, after your attempted bribery failed and you got your money back, what did you do with it?
MARCION	Well naturally, I invested it in my own church here in Rome.
TERTULLIAN	But why did you come to Rome in the first place?
MARCION	If you want to change the world, Tertullian, you have to go to its capital.
TERTULLIAN	Never give up, do you? But what made you think you would be able to change the world from Rome, something you obviously failed to do twice before?
MARCION	Rome is a great laboratory[22], my friend, a laboratory for great thinkers and men of vision, a centre for those on the quest for truth. Besides, Christianity here in Rome is purer, less falsified by Jewish elements, than it is in the East.[23] It was thus the perfect environment for us to grow.
TERTULLIAN	What do you mean 'us'?
MARCION	Me and my brothers, of course. Our community has been rapidly growing during the last few years.[24]
TERTULLIAN	It's an epidemic. Heretics only produce more heretics. And yet, in the end you will learn that you made the wrong choice. The Roman spirit, this admirable love for order and discipline, will be able to deal even with the most dangerous plague of heresy.[25]
MARCION	On what authority do you call us heretics, brother?
TERTULLIAN	On the authority of the Church!

MARCION	What is the Church, my friend? I only see a loose federation of Christian communities, without outward cohesion or inner unity of doctrine.[26]
TERTULLIAN	What about Anicetus[27]?
MARCION	What about him?
TERTULLIAN	You owe him allegiance. He is the bishop of Rome.
MARCION	He may be bishop of Rome, but he is not infallible.
TERTULLIAN	Oh, he is indeed. He just doesn't know it yet.
MARCION	Is this part of your Montanist glossolaly?
TERTULLIAN	I am not a Montanist! Although I admit that I do admire these people for their rigid asceticism and their strict practice of penance. But I am still a loyal son of the Church.[28] And Anicetus is in the rightful succession of the apostles.[29] He is the guardian of the rule of faith here in the capital.
MARCION	What is this rule of faith, Tertullian?
TERTULLIAN	The rule of faith is altogether one, alone immovable and irreformable, the rule of believing in one only God omnipotent, the Creator of the universe, and His Son Jesus Christ, born of the Virgin Mary, crucified under Pontius Pilate, raised again the third day from the dead, received in the heavens, sitting now at the right hand of the Father, destined to come to judge the living and the dead through the resurrection of the flesh.[30]
MARCION	And what if I told you that we have a rule of faith of our own? The rule of believing in one God perfectly good, superior to the God who created the universe, and His Son Jesus Christ,

who is not the one destined by the Creator to come at some time still future for the re-establishment of the Jewish state, not born, manifested in human form, abolishing the prophets and the Law, crucified under Pontius Pilate, raised again the third day from the dead.[31]

So we would both have a rule of faith. Who shall decide between us?

TERTULLIAN   Your rule is the more recent one.

MARCION   What is that supposed to mean?

TERTULLIAN   That which is of later importation must be reckoned heresy, because that has to be considered truth which was delivered of old and from the beginning. For in so far as the false is a corruption of the true, to that extent must the truth have preceded that which is false.[32]

MARCION   Well, in this case you have just condemned yourself, my friend. For my rule of faith goes back to the teaching of our Lord Jesus Christ and his one real apostle Paul. Yours on the other hand is a perverted mishmash, made up by false apostles and Jewish forgers.

TERTULLIAN   How dare you?! I'll ...

MARCION   (*making a conciliatory gesture*) Brother, it is late, and I see that the long journey has exhausted you. Why don't you just have some rest here in my house overnight, and we will talk about all this tomorrow?

TERTULLIAN   Are you out of your mind? What makes you think I would actually stay here with you?

MARCION   Well, you said you have come to investigate. Wouldn't the best way to do so be spending as much time with me as you can?

TERTULLIAN   (*hesitating*) Maybe you are right after all. I

	must say I'm surprised that you would have me stay here with you like this. Doesn't it bother you to have an investigator around?
MARCION	Not at all! I have nothing to hide. In fact, I am more than pleased to have the chance to introduce you to our community. Who knows, maybe your eyes will even be opened in the end.
TERTULLIAN	I will never join the enemy. Never!
MACION	Why do you see us as adversaries, Tertullian?
TERTULLIAN	Why?! You plan to rend our church and make a split in it forever![33]
MARCION	I never said anything like this! On the contrary, I still have hope that all this does not have to end in argument and discord. Polycarp is coming to Rome in a few days. I will request acceptance from him.
TERTULLIAN	Your optimism is truly admirable, although completely out of touch with reality. But I'll tell you something, I'm going to stay here with you until you meet the bishop of Smyrna. I wouldn't want to miss that for all the grain in Egypt.
MARCION	(*reaching out his hand to Tertullian*) Then it is agreed, brother, you shall be my guest for the next few days.
TERTULLIAN	(*taking Marcion's hand*) So be it, heretic!

Scene II

A fruitful discussion

The garden of Marcion's villa.

Marcion is picking apples from one of his trees. Enter Tertullian.

MARCION   Ah, good morning, brother. Did you have a
               good night's sleep?

TERTULLIAN   Your accommodation is indeed comfort-
               able.

MARCION   (*offering him an apple*) Would you like one?

TERTULLIAN   (*taking the apple and eating it*) These are really
               good apples.

MARCION   That's because they come from a good tree,
               my friend. As our Lord Jesus Christ said: *No
               good tree brings forth bad fruit, nor does a bad
               tree bring forth good fruit.*[34]

TERTULLIAN   So he said indeed. For he knew that a good
               mind does not produce evil actions, nor an
               evil mind such as yours good ones.[35]

MARCION   I wonder if that's really what he wanted to say.

TERTULLIAN   What else? The parable is most simple and
               evident.

MARCION   Well, let me put it this way: consider the
               world, what do you see?

TERTULLIAN   I see the magnificent creation of God, our fa-
               ther. A great work!

24

MARCION	(*sneering*) A great work indeed, and worthy of a God.[36]
TERTULLIAN	What are you saying?! You dare to despise the creation of our God?!
MARCION	The creation is only the bad fruit, I despise the bad tree, the Creator himself.
TERTULLIAN	I will not have this blasphemy going on like that!
MARCION	Come on, Tertullian, look at the world, it is pathetic.
TERTULLIAN	Pathetic? Just look around in this beautiful garden. (*Pointing at things in the garden*) There, imitate, if you can, this spider's network![37] Look at this beautiful little flower here! Think of a feather of a peacock or just of a moorcock. Do these things permit you to judge the Creator a low-grade artificer?[38]
MARCION	I am not concerned with animals or plants.[39] Look at the so-called pride of creation. Look into a mirror.
TERTULLIAN	I see the image and likeness of God.[40]
MARCION	All you see is a weak and mortal creature, a sinner! Why would a good God have created man like this?
TERTULLIAN	God did not create us this way, Adam's fall caused this disastrous situation.
MARCION	Then what kind of a God is he? If he was prescient, he would have foreseen that the fall would happen, if he was omnipotent, he could have prevented it from happening and if he was truly good, he would have done so.[41]
TERTULLIAN	So, you are nothing but an Epicurean[42] dog, growling against the truth of God![43]

MARCION	You don't need an Epicurus to figure these things out, my friend. They are obvious to every human intellect.
TERTULLIAN	Except to those of thousands of devout Christians throughout the Empire!
MARCION	Very well then, how can you explain the fall without denying God's foreknowledge, omnipotence or goodness?
TERTULLIAN	Since it could not have happened from God's side, the reason must be found in the constitution of man. As I said, man was created in God's image and likeness, which means, he was created with power to choose, and power to act for himself. He was created as a free man.[44] Therefore, the fall is completely imputable to man's own choice. Did you ever hear Adam blame his Creator saying: 'Thou hast not moulded me skilfully'?[45]
MARCION	Ha, the Creator didn't even know where Adam was. Like in a game of hide-and-seek he, the 'Omniscient', ran around in his own garden, calling: *Adam, where art thou*?
TERTULLIAN	You are such a smart alec! Do you really think God was ignorant of Adam's hiding-place? This question is not to be read in a simple manner, not with an interrogative intonation, 'Where art thou Adam?', but with an insistent and incisive and accusative tone, 'Adam where thou art!', which means 'Thou art in perdition', which means 'Thou art no longer here', so that the words spoken may end in reproof and in sorrow.[46]
MARCION	So, your God felt sorrow for not having intervened?

TERTULLIAN	He couldn't intervene! Once God had granted man freedom he must withdraw from his own freedom, restraining within himself that foreknowledge and superior power by which he might have been able to prevent man from using his freedom badly, and so falling into peril. If he had intervened, he would be an unstable, inconsistent and untrustworthy God.[47]
MARCION	And I'd still say he is, for he does intervene in other situations. Didn't he harden Pharaoh's heart? You see, Tertullian, your God does not grant men their free will, he treats people like marionettes. He did not intervene with Adam so that sin may enter the world, he did intervene with Pharaoh so that evil might prevail. Isn't that what your God meant when he said: *It is I who create evil?*[48]
TERTULLIAN	Your knowledge of Scripture is remarkable[49], I give you that. A pity you completely lack the skills of interpretation. First of all we have to distinguish two kinds of evil, evils of sin and evils of punishment. So the Creator's statement refers to those evils which appertain to a judge, which indeed are evil to those on whom they are inflicted, though on their own account they are good things because they are just things. God did harden Pharaoh's heart, but Pharaoh already deserved to be given to destruction, as having already denied God.[50]
MARCION	So you think of him as a fair judge then? Tell me, why does he punish the children for the sin of the fathers?[51] This seems hardly fair to

me. Why should I be punished for something my father did?

TERTULLIAN It was Israel's hardness which demanded remedies of that sort, to cause them to obey the divine Law at least through consideration for their posterity. For surely any man will be more concerned for his children's safety than for his own.[52]

MARCION And what if your father by any chance would not have been concerned for your safety and just went on with his sinful life? I suppose you would just love to be punished for something you are in no way responsible for?

TERTULLIAN Don't forget the words of Jeremiah: *In those days people will no longer say: The fathers have eaten sour grapes, and the children's teeth are set on edge*[53], which means that the father would not take upon him the son's sin, nor the son his father's sin, but that everyone would bear the guilt of his own sin.[54]

MARCION Aha, there he is, your stable, consistent and trustworthy God, changing his mind whenever he pleases. Just as he had forbidden stealing, and then personally ordered the Hebrews to steal gold and silver from the Egyptians.

TERTULLIAN That wasn't stealing! The Hebrews just demanded wages to be paid to them for that slave-labour, the drawing of the brick-kilns and the building of country houses. And, as a matter of fact, the compensation is still not adequate, if the labour of six hundred thousand men through all those years is priced at a penny a day each.[55]

MARCION	You can use your lawyer tricks all you like, but in the end you will have to admit that this God is as weak and unstable as his creatures, feeling emotions like anger, exasperation and even repentance. Doesn't one of his prophets say: *And God repented of the wickedness which he had said he would do unto them, and he did it not.*[56] Tell me how a God can feel repentant about his deeds?
TERTULLIAN	O you fool, who from things human form conjectures about things divine![57] How do you reckon there is in God something human, instead of everything divine?[58] God does possess these sensations, but in perfection, for he alone is perfect. He can be angry without being shaken, can be annoyed without coming into peril, can be moved without being overthrown.[59] And as to his repentance: God did indeed repent about his wickedness – by which his punishment as a judge is to be understood of course. But repentance in this case does not mean an admission of error, as it would be in human conditions. God saw that the Ninevites, whom he planned to punish for their sins, turned from their evil ways. Thus, his change of mind is directed by the occurrence of varying circumstances.[60]
MARCION	Circumstances he was obviously not able to foresee.
TERTULLIAN	Make up your mind! First you blame God for being evil, now you blame him for being merciful. Who are you to say 'God ought not to have done that', or 'He ought to have done this instead'? You believe yourself

better advised than God? Remember the prophet's words: *Who has known the mind of the Lord or who has been his counsellor?*[61]

MARCION   Ah, I see, now that you don't know what to say anymore, you come up with these platitudes.

Enter Apelles.

APELLES   My bishop, I think it is time.
MARCION   Yes, you are right. Thank you, brother Apelles.

Exit Apelles.

TERTULLIAN   Time for what?
MARCION   I have a little surprise for you.
TERTULLIAN   I am not very fond of surprises.
MARCION   Well, then I hope you will enjoy this one. Just follow me.
TERTULLIAN   I warn you ...

As they are leaving the garden, an apple falls down on Tertullian's head. Tertullian stops.

TERTULLIAN   (*as if in a trance*) Every object in the Universe attracts every other object with a force directed along the line of centres for the two objects that is proportional to the product of their masses and inversely proportional to the square of the separation between the two objects.
MARCION   (*aside*) And he calls me a smart alec.

30

Scene III

As good as it gets

The theatre.

TERTULLIAN	(*most angry*) I still can't believe you actually talked me into this!
MARCION	What is your problem now? We have some great seats.[62]
TERTULLIAN	I don't give a damn about the seats! I hate these idolatrous plays![63]
MARCION	It is not some primitive trash we are watching here[64], my friend. This is Sophocles' Antigone, a masterpiece.
TERTULLIAN	A masterpiece of distortion, perhaps. A play is nothing but the perverted use of the creation by the creatures![65] God, the author of truth, does not like the false. He will not approve of anyone who feigns voice, sex or age, or who pretends love, anger, groans or tears. Besides, as it is declared in his Law that a man who wears women's clothing is condemned[66], what will be his judgment of the pantomime, who is even trained to play a woman![67]

A (female sounding) voice from the stage:
'How savagely impious men use me,
For keeping a Law that is holy.' [68]

TERTULLIAN	See, that's exactly what I meant. But not only are these plays an offence to God's truth, they also incite passion in the spectators. They create rivalry, rage, bitterness, wrath or grief, which are all against our discipline.[69]
MARCION	I'm not so sure about that, brother. Doesn't Antigone's tragic fate rather remind you of the glorious Passion of our Lord Jesus Christ?
TERTULLIAN	I will never understand how you can believe in Christ, although you entirely disapprove of all the prophets who announced his coming.
MARCION	Very simple, because he is not the one announced by the prophets. Their Messiah is still to come. For the prophets expected a Messiah destined by the Creator to re-establish the Jewish state[70], a great political and military leader, a warrior.
TERTULLIAN	Where did you get that from?
MARCION	From the prophets themselves! Isaiah says: *Before the child knows how to say Father and Mother, he will take up the strength of Damascus and the spoils of Samaria against the king of the Assyrians.*[71]
TERTULLIAN	Do you really suppose the infant was going to call men to arms by his mewling, and give the signal for war with a rattle-box instead of a trumpet, and launch his attack upon the enemy not from horse or chariot or city-wall, but from his nurse's or nursemaid's shoulder or back, and thus obtain control of Damascus and Samaria in the place of his mother's breasts? (*sneering*) I am sure this might be possible among the barbarians of Pontus,

	whose children know how to handle a spear before they learn to chew. However, nature does not permit a man to learn warfare before life.[72]
MARCION	And what do you conclude from all that?
TERTULLIAN	That this statement by Isaiah must be taken as figurative.[73]
MARCION	Yes, of course. That's your solution to everything, isn't it? I can't handle the meaning of a statement, therefore it has to be meant allegorically.[74] Besides, in your evaluation you are just as arbitrary as your God, since nature does not permit a virgin to bear a child either, and yet you take the prophet literally in that case.[75]
TERTULLIAN	So you don't believe Christ was born of the Virgin Mary?
MARCION	I don't believe Christ was born at all! He is in no way connected to the dump of the Creator[76], and even less to the sewer of the womb[77], this filthy concretion of fluid and blood[78].
TERTULLIAN	I suppose you are also going to deny that he has come in the flesh, as John foretold the antichrist would.[79]
MARCION	I consider it most peculiar that you blame me for believing something which is clearly pointed out by our common master Paul[80], when he states that Christ was in the likeness of man[81]. And the Gospel, which we also both accept, plainly states that Christ slipped away through the midst of the crowd[82], something a human body could obviously not have done.
TERTULLIAN	It is true that he slipped away through the midst of them, but he could do so because,

33

as often happens, the crowd gave way, or was even broken up.[83] But tell me something else, you, who call yourself a loyal follower of the Apostle, don't you hear him declaring this the chief foundation of the Gospel, of our salvation and of his own preaching: *I delivered unto you, first of all, that Christ died for our sins, and that he was buried, and that he rose again the third day.*[84]

MARCION I do indeed hear this good news, apart from Christ dying for our sins.[85]

TERTULLIAN What do you mean?

MARCION Christ's death was not for the forgiveness of sins, but to redeem us from the Creator's claim[86], as the Apostle says: "Christ has redeemed us."[87]

TERTULLIAN But how can *you* speak of Christ's death?![88] If you deny his flesh, how can you affirm his death? For death is the particular experience of flesh, which by means of death is turned downwards into the earth from which it was taken.[89]

MARCION Yes, according to the rules of the flesh's pitiful Creator, your argument would certainly be conclusive. But you are not willing to see the utter newness of the Gospel. O wealth of riches! Folly, power and ecstasy! Seeing that there can be nothing to say about it, or to imagine about it; or to compare it to![90] Christ does not obey the rules of this world, and so his body was not composed of the material elements. But that doesn't mean that he was a mere ghost.

TERTULLIAN (*almost despairingly*) What was he, then?

MARCION	He is the self-revelation of God[91], the God of pure goodness and love, the good tree that brings forth good fruit.
TERTULLIAN	Aha, finally you belch all your heretic venom![92] First you try to destroy God the Creator, but even you cannot deny his being, for ever since things have existed, their Creator has become known along with them.[93] Therefore, as you were forced to admit his existence, you tried everything to slander him. But not only are you attacking our God, you even invent a second one of your own. Well, I guess to the drunk a single lamp just looks double.[94]
MARCION	I never thought I'd have to say this, but could you please display a little bit more seriousness?
TERTULLIAN	I must admit that I find it hard to take this matter seriously any more. Your claim is nothing but absurd. For all men's common sense will accept the definition that God is the *summum magnum*[95]. And since there is universal agreement on this, it follows from this definition that the *summum magnum* is of necessity singular, for surely it has nothing equal to it.[96] And so does the Christian truth clearly state: if God is not one, he does not exist.[97]
MARCION	So that's it for you, right? A pedantic philosophical definition[98] and a perverted recent tradition make you shut your eyes to the most obvious, the fact that the God revealed in our Lord Jesus Christ, the God of the glorious Gospel, this perfectly good God can not be same as the God whom the Law and

Prophets spoke of, the maker of this pitiful world, who admits himself that he creates evil, who constantly changes his mind and contradicts himself, this ignorant and emotional fool, this cruel judge.[99]

TERTULLIAN So, you proudly present a new God to the world. Ha, just like a schoolboy who is proud of his new shoes.[100]

MARCION What did I tell you about seriousness?

TERTULLIAN Come on, don't you see how irrational this is? What new God is there, except a false one?[101]

MARCION Is this your famous definition again that oldness guarantees truth?[102] (*sneering*) I certainly bow to this most evident logic.

If you were willing to except the Gospel as your authority instead, you would find that Christ himself declares: *No one knows who the Son is except the Father, and no one knows who the Father is except the Son and those to whom the Son shall reveal him.*[103] Therefore, it must have been a new, formerly unknown God whom Christ preached.

TERTULLIAN Alright then, who is this new God of yours? What does he do? You call our God the Creator and blame him for having created an unworthy world, but how much more unworthy is it not to have created anything at all![104] Where are the works of your God, heretic?

MARCION One work is sufficient to our God, that he has delivered man by his supreme and most excellent goodness.[105] He revealed himself in Jesus Christ, so that everyone who believes in him will be saved.[106] Watch with amazement

	our God's perfect goodness: he willingly and liberally expanded his love upon strangers without any obligation of kinship.[107]
TERTULLIAN	But tell me this, if your God is all that good, why did he bring himself into notice so lately, why has his goodness not been in operation from the beginning?[108] Why didn't he rescue man from the 'malice' of the Creator earlier?
MARCION	Please remind me, how long did your God wait until he rescued his people from the hand of the Egyptians?
TERTULLIAN	Don't be ridiculous!
MARCION	You are the ridiculous one! A short while ago you claimed that only a fool would say things like 'God ought not to have done that', or 'He ought to have done this instead', now you say them yourself. You blamed me for forming conjectures from things human about things divine, and now you seriously think that God is subject to our human ideas of time and space?
TERTULLIAN	And what about you? You blame our God for not having intervened to prevent Adam's fall, and yet your God let hundreds of generations perish without interfering.
MARCION	You believe in Christ's descent into Hades, don't you?
TERTULLIAN	I believe in the tradition of our Church![109]
MARCION	Very well, then you should see that our God did not let our ancestors perish. Christ descended into Hades to save them.
TERTULLIAN	You mean he saved our noble ancestors such as Abel, Noah and Abraham?

MARCION   What? Don't you get anything? Christ saved
               those who believe in him, not these pitiful
               lackeys of the Creator. All who ran to him,
               even Cain, the men of Sodom and the Egyp-
               tians, he took into his kingdom.[110]

An angry voice from behind:
'Will you be quiet! There are people trying to watch the play here!'

MARCION   (*to the man behind him*) Of course, I'm so
               sorry.
               Maybe we should continue our conversation
               at my place.
TERTULLIAN   Agreed.

Scene IV

Canon-Ball

Marcion's private library.

Tertullian is looking at Marcion's books.

TERTULLIAN	You have quite an impressive collection here. What a pity that an educated man such as yourself[111] had to fall for such a foolish heresy.
MARCION	You sure don't make it easy to know whether I should feel flattered or offended.
TERTULLIAN	(*surprised*) What's this? You even have a copy of the Law and the Prophets here? I thought you would rather see that burned.
MARCION	Why would I? These texts are most valuable to me.[112] They clearly reveal the character flaws of the Creator, the God of the Jewish nation[113]. And they thus prove that he cannot be the same as the God revealed in Christ.
TERTULLIAN	Yes, heard that before. You really need some new material.
MARCION	So then how about this? (*handing him a book from the shelf*) This is a work of my own. I call it the *Antitheses*.
TERTULLIAN	(*taking the book and leafing through it*) It's a pretty long work. Are you listing the contradictions of your own nonsense in it?
MARCION	Actually, I'm trying to demonstrate the opposition between the Jewish Scriptures and the

	Gospel[114] by juxtaposing contrary statements of the two[115]. And there are quite a few!
TERTULLIAN	Give me one!
MARCION	Very well[116]: the Law of the Creator forbids to do any work on the Sabbath, and he even ordered to put a man to death, just because he was gathering sticks on that day.[117] Whereas our Lord Jesus Christ subverted the Sabbath[118] by allowing his disciples to pluck some heads of grain and eat them this very day.[119]
TERTULLIAN	As before, your disdain for the sacred Scriptures has obviously prevented you from reading them correctly. The Law says about the Sabbath: *In it thou shalt do no manner of work, except that which is to be done for every soul.*[120] Therefore, Christ did in no way revoke the Sabbath, but retained the Law of it when he performed a work for his disciples' soul by granting to hungry men the comfort of food. And by this and by so many others of his actions, our Lord Jesus Christ proved his word: *I have not come to abolish the Law but to fulfil it.*[121]
MARCION	He never said anything like that! Christ is the end of the Law![122]
TERTULLIAN	Hand me the Gospel according to Matthew.
MARCION	There is no such thing as a Gospel according to somebody![123] There is only the one Gospel of Christ!
TERTULLIAN	Well, obviously. But there are still four men who preached the Gospel. The apostles John and Matthew introduced faith to us, and Luke and Mark, being followers of the apostles, gave it renewal.[124]

40

MARCION	Their diversity does not make you think?
TERTULLIAN	Not as long as there is agreement on the essentials of faith – and on these they show no agreement with you![125]
MARCION	That's because they are falsified! The Apostle clearly stated that there is only one Gospel, when he wrote to the Galatians: *I am astonished that you are so quickly deserting the one who called you in the grace of Christ and are turning to a different Gospel; not that there is another Gospel, but some people are throwing you into confusion and are trying to pervert the Gospel of Christ.*[126] (*handing him another book from the shelf*) Here, this is the true Gospel of Christ.
TERTULLIAN	(*taking the book and leafing through it*) It looks like the Gospel according to Luke[127], but a lot of passages seem to be lost. Look here, the complete beginning is missing.
MARCION	Obviously, since Christ was neither born of Mary nor was he in any way linked to John the Baptist, this pathetic pawn of the Creator.
TERTULLIAN	So where did you find this mutilated version of the Gospel?
MARCION	I produced it myself.
TERTULLIAN	What?!
MARCION	Well, I am not the actual author, of course. But it was me who re-established its original form by cleaning it from all these judaistic interpolations.
TERTULLIAN	What are you talking about?!
MARCION	You mean you don't know about the great judaistic conspiracy, brother? How can you be unaware of it? The Apostle himself stated that

false brothers had infiltrated their ranks.[128] These partisans of the Creator[129] perverted the Gospel of Christ by smuggling references to the Law and the Prophets into it, thereby suggesting that Christ belonged to the Creator.[130]

TERTULLIAN (*looking upwards*) O Christ, most patient Lord, who didst bear so many years with this interference of thy preaching, until Marcion forsooth came to thy rescue.[131]

MARCION No blasphemy please. All honour belongs to Christ and his one true apostle Paul, who revealed the new God to us through his missionary work.

TERTULLIAN I'm going to tell you this one last time now: the God of the Jewish Scriptures and the God of the Gospel is one and the same! Paul did not announce a new God!

MARCION Then why was he chosen by Christ when he was already at rest in heaven?[132] Obviously because the former apostles had failed. Paul himself attacked Peter and the other pillars of the apostleship for not walking uprightly according to the truth of the Gospel.[133]

TERTULLIAN I do not deny that Paul was opposed to Judaism, which becomes indeed most obvious in his letter to the Galatians. And it is with open arms that we receive all that abolition of the ancient Law.[134] So, when the Apostle said to them: *I am astonished that you are so quickly deserting the one who called you in the grace of Christ and are turning to a different Gospel,* he meant another in rule of conduct, not in divinity. Thus, he only criticized Peter for

	inconsistency in his taking of food. For the Gospel of Christ calls everyone away from the Law, towards grace, but not away from the Creator towards another God.[135]
MARCION	But the Law is the Law of the Creator. Being called away from the Law means being called away from him. How could there be continuity between a harsh Law and a most merciful love?
TERTULLIAN	God himself, through his prophet, announced that there would be a great change: *The old things are passed away, behold these are new things that I make*[136].
MARCION	Let there be new things, I don't mind. But I deny any change in God. That is why the Law and the Gospel cannot have the same author. That is why it was my duty to continue Paul's fight against the forgers, by erasing all the references to the Law and the Prophets[137] within the Gospel and the letters of the Apostle[138]. I re-edited both sources in their pure form so that they may be a canon for our church.[139]
TERTULLIAN	A canon, what do you mean?
MARCION	This collection of texts will form the guideline for all our teaching. I call it the *New Testament*.[140]
TERTULLIAN	The New Heresy, you mean! I must say, I've met a few heretics in my life, but I have never seen such fanaticism. Do you really think you are the chosen one?! You expunge all these passages just because they happen to oppose your peculiar view[141], you edit mutilated versions of the texts, and call it a binding guideline?

MARCION	I do by no means claim infallibility in this matter. I just started this most holy task of bringing the Gospel back to its true light. My followers will continue what I began.[142]
TERTULLIAN	You consider yourself faithful to the Gospel? Don't you see your bias? You are at war against the Law and the Prophets, just because you have, despite all evidence, this crazy obsession with an antagonism between them and the Gospel.
MARCION	An antagonism which is evident in the Scriptures themselves.
TERTULLIAN	Okay, I can see it's no use. You are nothing but a Pontic Mouse gnawing away the Gospel.[143]
MARCION	Better than a Carthaginian beaver constructing a dam against the truth.
TERTULLIAN	There are no beavers in Africa!
MARCION	Alright, you win.

Scene V

Marcionus Gnosticus?

On the street.

TERTULLIAN   Ah, the streets of Rome. The city is as magnificent as it ever was.

MARCION   So why is it that you don't dwell here any more?

TERTULLIAN   I don't know. (*cuttingly*) Maybe it's the people who are living in Rome these days.

MARCION   Speaking of those, look who's coming towards us. It's Ptolemaeus[144].

TERTULLIAN   The Gnostic leader? Oh no. One heretic at a time, please!

MARCION   Too late.

Enter Ptolemaeus.

PTOLEMAEUS   My, my, who have we here? The mighty bishop and his friend.

TERTULLIAN   I'm not his friend! And he's not a bishop!

PTOLEMAEUS   Aggressive, aren't we?

TERTULLIAN   You better watch out, Ptolemaeus! My aggression might soon turn against you!

PTOLEMAEUS   I see your choice of friends has not improved much, Marcion.

MARCION   Just because I don't exclusively hang out with pseudo-intellectuals[145] and rich women[146]? Tertullian here may not be Mr. Sunshine, but

	at least he is not as condescending as you are.
TERTULLIAN	You are siding with me? I thought you guys were actually two of a kind.
PTOLEMAEUS	Well, I once thought that he might be one of us. But his mind is closed to the true *Gnosis*.
MARCION	That's because I'm faithful to the Gospel!
PTOLEMAEUS	Faithful? Don't make me laugh! Which one of us used a knife to commit murder of Scripture by changing it arbitrarily according to his own view?[147]
TERTULLIAN	Hey, this guy isn't so bad after all!
MARCION	I only did what had to be done by erasing all false interpolations within the holy texts. I did not invent an absurd mythological system.
PTOLEMAEUS	It is absurd to you and your kind. We Gnostics know about the Pleroma of thirty Aeons which emanated from *Bythos*.[148]
MARCION	And you consider this nonsense to be based on Scripture?
PTOLEMAEUS	Indeed I do. Remember the parable of the workers in the vineyard. Certain workers were hired at the first hour, others at the third, others at the sixth, others at the ninth, others at the eleventh. Added together these hours give a total of thirty.[149] See, this clearly signifies the thirty Aeons.

Marcion and Tertullian look at each other. Marcion gestures 'crazy'.

PTOLEMAEUS	(*complacently laughing*) Ah, jealousy, the green-eyed monster which doth mock the meat it feeds on.

	But I can live with that. What is mockery of commoners compared to my special knowledge? I have the divine spark within me, the semen of election. 'From the beginning we are immortal and children of eternal life'[150], as my Master Valentinus[151] used to say.
TERTULLIAN	Well, now that you are so much smarter then we are, would you mind telling us where you know all that from?
PTOLEMAEUS	It was the call of Jesus![152] Through him we became aware of our situation that we are not of this world. (*looking upwards*) Oh *Logos*, take me home to the place I belong.
TERTULLIAN	So, you have this absurd idea too about a God who is separated from this world?
PTOLEMAEUS	Not completely separated.[153] All things come from the good and perfect God, the one ingenerate Father. And so does the Demiurge, the Creator of this world, who is an image of the superior God.[154]
TERTULLIAN	(*to Marcion*) So he *is* like you in some ways.
MARCION	I'm nothing like him! I believe that Christ came for the salvation of everyone who believes in him, not to give a certain group of people some special knowledge.
PTOLEMAEUS	Don't worry, at least you belong to the psychic class, so there might be hope for you after all.
MARCION	You are a fool! There are no different classes of people. We were all made by the Creator, and we were made weak and mortal.[155] Only the infinite grace of God granted us redemption.
TERTULLIAN	I must admit that I'm puzzled about your friction. (*to Marcion*) I thought you were taught by the Gnostic Cerdo[156]?

MARCION	I knew him. But ...
PTOLEMAEUS	But when he saw that there was no knowledge in you, he gave you up, right?
MARCION	My teaching may not be based on some strange esoteric stuff, but it is plain and coherent.
PTOLEMAEUS	You really think so? Then please tell me, how can you attribute the Law, which does away with wrongdoing, to the injustice of the devil?[157]
MARCION	(*to Tertullian*) See, he has actually more in common with you. Both of you are constantly trying to distort my teaching. *(to Ptolemaeus)* I attribute the Law to the Creator, just as you do.[158] You were the one to invent a third figure, the adversary.
TERTULLIAN	Wait, wait, this is getting too much for me now!
PTOLEMAEUS	I know it must be hard for you to deal with things which are so much beyond your common understanding. Well, I'm afraid I'll have to go now.
MARCION	To one of your high society meetings, no doubt. (*sarcastically*) Well, have a nice evening.
PTOLEMAEUS	*(leaving)* May the Gnosis be with you!

Exit Ptolemaeus.

TERTULLIAN	Well, I never thought this would be possible, but he is even crazier than you.
MARCION	So you think there's hope for me?
TERTULLIAN	Dream on, heretic! The Church will never accept you. Polycarp will settle this matter once and for all.

MARCION	By the way, I heard he is coming tomorrow.
TERTULLIAN	I can hardly wait.
MARCION	While we do, I would be honoured if you would join me for diner.
TERTULLIAN	A condemned man's last meal? I'll give you that honour.

Scene VI

Alcohol, women and other vices

Marcion's villa. The triclinium.

Marcion and Tertullian are lying around a table.

MARCION	Nunc est bibendum! Only water, of course.[159]
TERTULLIAN	And we are not having any meat either, I suppose?
MARCION	You can have fish if you like.
TERTULLIAN	Do you really consider this a holier kind of food?[160]
MARCION	At least I do not follow all the 387 laws on food your God issued.
TERTULLIAN	I told you that the Jewish food laws do not apply to us.
MARCION	Ah, I see. It's your arbitrariness again. I keep what I like and don't care about the rest. Strange, considering that the entire Law was given by one and the same God.
TERTULLIAN	I remember, you and Ptolemaeus both consider the Law to be given by the Creator. Tell me then, is the Law evil?
MARCION	By no means! The Law is holy, and its commandment is righteous and good.[161]
TERTULLIAN	Now I'm puzzled. If you have such reverence for the Creator's Law, how can you try to destroy the Creator himself?[162]
MARCION	I do appreciate the Law insofar as it is directed

against evil, for our God condemns it too.[163] But the Creator did not give his Law to man in order to prevent evil, but on the contrary, so that trespass might increase[164], as the Apostle clearly states. Shame on this Lawgiver! He himself created man weak and frail and yet he puts this burden upon him and even dares to judge man according to this unrealizable Law.

TERTULLIAN God would not have laid the weight of the Law upon man, if the Law had been burdensome and man too feeble to bear it.[165] You have to accept that God endowed man with free will, for no Law could have been imposed upon one who had not in his own power the submission due to the Law. Nor could punishment be attached to transgression, unless contempt of the Law could have been blamed upon man's freedom of choice.[166]

MARCION Exactly, that is why our God does not punish.

TERTULLIAN Didn't you say that he condemns evil?

MARCION Of course he does.

TERTULLIAN So then why does he not punish it?!

MARCION Because he does not want to be feared. Only a bad God is to be feared, a good God is to be loved.[167]

TERTULLIAN A seductive thought, I admit. For what greater seduction is there than to abstain from punishing wrongdoing?[168] Well, I assume your wish was father to that thought. But tell me something else. If you are never punished by your God because he is all that good, what keeps you from boiling over into all manner of lust?[169]

MARCION Good Heavens! Never!

51

TERTULLIAN	So you do fear sin and therefore the one who forbids it.
MARCION	By no means!
TERTULLIAN	But why else would you restrain from sin?!
MARCION	Sin is sin, brother, punishment or no punishment. Is this really your idea of a relationship with God? Being a scared pawn before a frightening avenger who is constantly to be satisfied by your own merits?[170]
TERTULLIAN	You have to stop this black-and-white thinking. God is revealed both as Father and as Lord, as Father to be loved in affection, as Lord to be necessarily feared. He is to be loved because he prefers the sinner's repentance to his death, he is to be feared because he dislikes the sinners who do not repent. Therefore the Law lays down both these commandments: *Thou shalt love God*, and, *Thou shalt fear God*. The one it sets before the obedient, the other before the transgressor.[171]
MARCION	Your careful distinctions are indeed remarkable. But in the end you are just once more trying to reconcile things which simply don't go together. There is no room for fear in love.
TERTULLIAN	Maybe you should rather start developing some love for this world and the people in it. Is it true that you completely forbid your church members to marry?
MARCION	Well, not everybody can love the people of this world so much as your admired patriarchs to live in polygamy and keep concubines.
TERTULLIAN	There are certain practises which were necessary in former times and which afterwards

	had to be abrogated or modified.[172] But there is no reason to forbid marriage completely. [173]
MARCION	I thought you valued chastity very highly too.
TERTULLIAN	I give chastity preference, but only as a better thing over a good one, not as a good thing over a bad one.[174] Why do you condemn marriage in general?
MARCION	It was the Creator who ordered men to increase and multiply, so that he might execute his pitiful reign over mankind. We refuse to promote his creation.
TERTULLIAN	And you seriously think that this suppression of the whole increase of the human race is the will of a good God? How can he desire the salvation of the man whom he forbids to be born?[175]
MARCION	If it was the same God who gives you this life and salvation, why would he send his people through this miserable life first?
TERTULLIAN	So the meaning of life for you and your companions in misery[176] seems to be waiting for death, hoping for the kingdom of God in an eternal and heavenly possession.[177] Say, what is going to happen on the final day to those who do not believe in your God?
MARCION	They will be cast away out of sight of our God.[178]
TERTULLIAN	You mean there is actually an act of punishment on the part of your no-judgement-knowing God?
MARCION	This is no punishment. It is obvious that only those are saved who want to be saved. Those who stick to the Creator have excluded themselves from salvation.

TERTULLIAN	Oh what a God is this? Everywhere perverse, nowhere rational, in all aspects vain, and so nonexistent![179]
MARCION	We shall see what Polycarp thinks of all that. Maybe he will be more understanding than you are.
TERTULLIAN	You don't seem to be nervous at all about tomorrow. Don't you want to prepare yourself a little bit?
MARCION	I'm tired. But I like to think things through when I'm lying down.
	Weary with toil, I haste me to my bed,
	The dear repose for limbs with travel tired;
	But then begins a journey in my head
	To work my mind, when body's work's expired.
TERTULLIAN	Horace?
MARCION	Shakespeare.

Scene VII

The Showdown

The home of Anicetus.

Anicetus is waiting in the atrium. Enter Polycarp.

ANICETUS   Welcome to my humble home, Polycarp, most worthy bishop of Smyrna.

POLYCARP   I salute you, Anicetus, most worthy bishop of Rome, and offer you my gratitude for receiving me here in the City.[180]

ANICETUS   It is a great honour to provide for a disciple of the apostle John.[181]

POLYCARP   The honour is mine to meet the keeper of the tradition in the capital. I really hope we will be able to settle the dispute about the day of the Passover.[182]

Enter Tertullian.

TERTULLIAN   We have more urgent matters to attend to!

POLYCARP   What do you mean, brother?

TERTULLIAN   We have a new enemy: Marcion of Sinope.

ANICETUS   Ha, we have already rejected this heretic about ten years ago.

POLYCARP   These Gnostics are indeed a real nuisance, but we will turn many away from these heretics and bring them back to the church of God by proclaiming that from the apostles we have

55

	received this one and only truth transmitted by the church.[183]
TERTULLIAN	The Gnostics are a just a small exclusive bunch of weirdoes. Marcion is far more dangerous, he is so close to our church in many ways.[184] His community is like a dark reflection of the Church.
POLYCARP	Is the dark side stronger?
TERTULLIAN	No, no, no. Quicker, easier, more seductive. Marcion was clever in perceiving the complicated questions Christians have and offered radical and simple answers to them. His teaching, albeit absurd, is fascinating to the masses, and the number of his followers is growing every day. I just spent some days with him and I must say the worst thing is: he is utterly sincere in all that he's doing.
ANICETUS	The most dangerous heretics are those whose lives are good.[185] Nevertheless, we finally excommunicated him, and that's that.
TERTULLIAN	(*to Polycarp*) He is about to come here to seek acceptance from you.
POLYCARP	I'm afraid he is not in for a warm welcome.
ANICETUS	This is indeed a fateful hour. (*to Polycarp*) Tertullian is right. We have to put down all our differences and unite against him.[186]
POLYCARP	So be it.
TERTULLIAN	Here he comes.

Enter Marcion and Apelles.

MARCION	Greetings, beloved brothers in Christ.
TERTULLIAN	You may dispense with the pleasantries, heretic. Just state your business!

MARCION	Well, since you illustrious gentlemen desire a clear declaration, let me ask you this, what does this statement by our Saviour mean: They do not put new wine into old skins?[187]
ANICETUS	Child, the old skins represent the hearts of the Pharisees and scribes, inveterate in sins and unreceptive of the preaching of the Gospel.[188]
MARCION	That is not true. He wants to say that the new Gospel he is preaching cannot be in continuity with the old Law.
TERTULLIAN	You are puffed up with old wineskins, and befuddled with new wine, and consequently have sewn the patch of heretical newness upon the old Gospel.[189]
MARCION	Very well, no more discussion. Polycarp, most worthy bishop of Smyrna, here I stand, I can do no other: Recognize us!
POLYCARP	I recognize thee, as the firstborn of Satan.[190]
APELLES	How dare you?! One day my master will be glorified and will take his rightful place at the left hand of Christ in heaven, together with Paul at Christ's right hand.[191]
MARCION	Enough, Apelles. We shall retreat for now. But you haven't seen the last of us yet. Our church will continue to grow.
TERTULLIAN	I doubt it. Your own ban on procreation will take care of that.[192]
MARCION	Even if the time may not be ready yet, one day my teachings will rise again.
TERTULLIAN	And where might that be?
MARCION	In Germania.
TERTULLIAN	Germania? The only country in the world more barbaric than your own home of Pontus?

MARCION	The Germans are not to be underestimated. One day they will be a glorious nation of scholars.
TERTULLIAN	(*sneering*) Yes, of course. And then, I suppose, a German is going to be bishop of Rome too.
MARCION	With God all things are possible.

Abbreviations

Adv. haer. = Adversus haereses, *Irenaeus*

Adv. Marc. = Adversus Marcionem, *Tertullian*

Apol. = Apologia, *Justin*

Carn. = De carne Christi, *Tertullian*

Comm. Os. = Commentarii in Osee, *Jerome*

Comm. Rom. = Commentarii in epistulam ad Romanos, *Origen*

Ezek. Hom. = In Ezechielem homiliae, *Origen*

Herm. = Adversus Hermogenem, *Tertullian*

Ep. = Epistulae, *Jerome*

Hist. eccl. = Historia ecclesiastica, *Eusebius*

Hom. Luc. = In Lucam homiliae, *Origen*

Pan. = Panarion, *Epiphanius*

Praescr. = De praescriptione, *Tertullian*

Princ. = De principiis, *Origen*

Rec. = De recta in Deum fide

Ref. = Refutatio, *Hippolytus*

Spec. = De spectaculis, *Tertullian*

Ux. = Ad uxorem, *Tertullian*

Virg. = De virginibus velandis, *Tertullian*

Bibliography

Texts

De recta in Deum fide, in: Kenji Tsutsui. Die Auseinandersetzung mit den Markioniten im Adamantios-Dialog. Berlin: de Gruyter, 2004, p. 295-345.

Epiphanius. *Panarion. Vol. 2 (34-64)*. Herausgegeben von Karl Holl/Jürgen Dummer. GCS 31. Berlin: Akademie-Verlag, ²1980.

Eusèbe de Césarée. *Histoire ecclésiastique*. Traduction et annotation par Gustave Bardy. SC 31/41. Paris: Cerf, 1952/1955.

Hieronymus. *Commentarii in Prophetas minores*. CCSL 76. Turnholti: Brepols, 1969.

–. *Epistulae. Pars III. Epistulae CXXI-CLIV*. Edidit Isidorus Hilberg. CSEL 56. Vindobonae: Verlag der Österreichischen Akademie der Wissenschaften, 1996.

Hippolytus. *Refutatio omnium haeresium*. Edited by Miroslav Marcovich. PTS 25. Berlin: de Gruyter, 1986.

Irénée de Lyon. *Contre les hérésies I/III*. Edition critique par Adelin Rousseau/Louis Doutreleau. SC 264/211. Paris: Cerf, 1979/1974.

Justin. *Apologies*. Introduction, texte critique, traduction, commentaire et index par André Wartelle. Paris: Etudes Augustiniennes, 1987.

Origène. *Homélies sur Saint Luc*. Introduction, traduction et notes par Henri Crouzel/Francois Fournier/Pierre Perichon. SC 87. Paris: Cerf ,1962.

–. *Homélies sur Ezéchiel*. Introduction, traduction et notes par Marcel Borret. SC 352. Paris: Cerf, 1989.

–. *Vier Bücher von den Prinzipien*. Herausgegeben, übersetzt, mit kritischen und erläuternden Anmerkungen versehen von Herwig Görgemanns/Heinrich Karpp. Darmstadt: Wissenschaftliche Buchgesellschaft, ³1992.

–. *Commentarii in epistulam ad Romanos*. Übersetzt und eingeleitet von Theresia Heither. FC 2,3. Freiburg: 1993.

Prologus secundum Iohannem, in: Jürgen Regul. Die antimarcionitischen Evanglienprologe. Freiburg: Herder, 1969, p. 34f.

Tertullianus. *Opera*. CCSL 1/2. Turnholti: Brepols, 1954.

–. *Adversus Marcionem*. Edited and translated by Ernest Evans. Oxford: Clarendon Press, 1972.

Secondary Sources

Aland, Barbara. "Marcion: Versuch einer neuen Interpretation". *Zeitschrift für Theologie und Kirche* 70 (1973), p. 420-447.

–. Art. "Marcion". *Theologische Realenzyklopädie* 22 (1992), p. 89-101.

D'Alès, Adhémar. *La théologie de Tertullien*. Paris: Beauchesne, [2]1905.

Barnes, Timothy. *Tertullian: a historical and literary study*. Oxford: Clarendon Press, [2]1985.

Barth, Ferdinand. "Theater". *Theologische Realenzyklopädie* 33 (2001), p. 175-195.

Barton, John. "Marcion Revisited", in: Lee Martin McDonald/ James A. Sanders (ed.) *The Canon debate*. Peabody: Hendrickson Publishers, 2002, p. 341-354.

Bauer, Walter. *Rechtgläubigkeit und Ketzerei im ältesten Christentum*. Tübingen: Mohr, [2]1964.

Beck, Alexander. *Römisches Recht bei Tertullian und Cyprian*. Halle: Max Niemeyer. 1930.

Bianchi, Ugo. "Marcion: Theologien Biblique ou Docteur Gnostique?". *Vigiliae Christianae* 21 (1967), p. 141-149.

Blackman, Edwin Cyril. *Marcion and his Influence*. London: SPCK 1948.

Bousset, Wilhelm. *Hauptprobleme der Gnosis*. Göttingen: Vandenhoeck & Ruprecht, 1907.

Braun, René. *Deus Christianorum: recherches sur le vocabulaire doctrinal de Tertullien*. Paris: Etudes Augustiniennes, [2]1977.

Campenhausen, Hans Freiherr von. *Die Entstehung der christlichen Bibel*. Tübingen: Mohr, 1968.

Cancik, Hubert. "Gnostiker in Rom. Zur Religionsgeschichte der Stadt Rom im 2. Jahrhundert nach Christus", in: Jacob Taubes (ed.) *Gnosis und Politik*. München: Wilhelm Fink, 1984, p. 163-184.

Cook, John Manuel. *The Greeks in Ionia and the East*. London: Thames and Hudson, 1962.

Deakle, David. "Harnack & Cerdo", in: Gerhard May/Katharina Greschat (ed.) *Marcion und seine kirchengeschichtliche Wirkung*. Berlin: de Gruyter, 2002, p. 177-190.

Enslin, Morton. "The Pontic Mouse". *Anglican Theological Review* 27 (1945), p. 1-16.

De Faye. Eugène. *Gnostiques et gnosticisme*. Paris: Geuthner, [2]1925.

Foerster, Werner. "Die Grundzüge der Ptolemäischen Gnosis". *New Testament Studies* 6 (1960), p. 16-31.

Gager, John. "Marcion and Philosophy". *Vigiliae Christianae* 26 (1972), p. 53-59.

Georges, Karl Ernst. *Ausführliches Lateinisch-Deutsches Handwörterbuch I*. Darmstadt: Wissenschaftliche Buchgesellschaft, ⁸1998.

Hall, Stuart G. "Marcion". *A Dictionary of Biblical Interpretation*. London: SCM Press, 1990, p. 422-424.

Hallonsten, Gösta. *Satisfactio bei Tertullian*. Malmö: CWK Gleerup, 1984.

–. *Meritum bei Tertullian*. Malmö: CWK Gleerup, 1985.

Harnack, Adolf von. *Mission und Ausbreitung des Christentums*. Leipzig: Hinrich, 1902.

–. *Marcion. Das Evangelium vom fremden Gott*. Darmstadt: Wissenschaftliche Buchgesellschaft, ²1996.

–. *Marcion. Der moderne Gläubige des 2. Jahrhunderts, der erste Reformator. Die Dorpater Preisschrift (1870)*. Edited by Friedemann Steck, Berlin: de Gruyter, 2003.

Hoffmann, Joseph. *Marcion: on the restitution of Christianity*. Chico: Scholars Press, 1984.

Hofmann, Johannes. "Die amtliche Stellung der in der ältesten römischen Bischofsliste überlieferten Männer in der Kirche von Rom". *Historisches Jahrbuch* 109 (1989), p. 1-23.

Kinzig, Wolfram. "Kainh. diaqh,kh: The Title of the New Testament in the second and third centuries". *Journal of Theological Studies* 45 (1994), p. 519-544.

Knox, John. *Marcion and the New Testament.* Chicago: University of Chicago Press, 1942.

Koch, Ernst. "Höllenfahrt Christi". *Theologische Realenzyklopädie* 15 (1986), p. 455-461.

Kunkel, Wolfgang. *Die römischen Juristen.* Köln: Böhlau, ²2001.

Lampe, Peter. *Die stadtrömischen Christen in den ersten beiden Jahrhunderten.* Tübingen: Mohr, 1987.

–. "Anicetus". *Religion in Geschichte und Gegenwart* 1 (1998), p. 503.

La Piana, George. "The Roman Church at the end of the second century". *Harvard Theological Review* 18 (1925), p. 201-277.

Layton, Bentley. *The Gnostic Scriptures.* New York: Doubleday, 1987.

Löhr, Winrich A. "La doctrine de Dieu dans la lettre a Flora de Ptolémée". *Revue d'Histoire et de Philosophie religieuses* 75 (1995), p. 177-191.

–. "Die Auslegung des Gesetzes bei Markion, den Gnostikern und den Manichäern", in: Georg Schöllgen/ Clemens Scholten (ed.) *Stimuli. Exegese und ihre Hermeneutik in Antike und Christentum. Festschrift für Ernst Dassmann.* Münster: Aschendorff, 1996, p. 77-95.

–. "Did Marcion distinguish between a just and a good God?", in: Gerhard May/Katharina
Greschat (ed.) *Marcion und seine kirchengeschichtliche Wirkung.* Berlin: de Gruyter, 2002, p. 131-146.

Markschies, Christoph. *Valentinus Gnosticus?*. Tübingen: Mohr, 1992.

–. "Die valentianische Gnosis und Marcion – einige neue Perspektiven", in: Gerhard May/Katharina Greschat (ed.) *Marcion und seine kirchengeschichtliche Wirkung*. Berlin: de Gruyter, 2002, p. 159-175.

May, Gerhard. "Ein neues Markionbild?". *Theologische Rundschau* 51 (1986), p. 404-413.

–. "Der Streit zwischen Petrus und Paulus in Antiochien bei Markion", in: Walter Homolka/Otto Ziegelmeier (ed.) *Von Wittenberg nach Memphis. Festschrift für Reinhard Schwarz*. Göttingen: Vandenhoeck & Ruprecht, 1989, p. 204-211.

Meijering, Eginhard Peter. *Tertullian contra Marcion: Gotteslehre in der Polemik*. Leiden: Brill, 1977.

Norelli, Enrico. "Marcion: ein christlicher Philosoph oder ein Christ gegen die Philosophie?", in: Gerhard May/Katharina Greschat (ed.) *Marcion und seine kirchengeschichtliche Wirkung*. Berlin: de Gruyter, 2002, p. 114-130.

Powell, Douglas. "Tertullianists and Cataphrygians". *Vigiliae Christianae* 29 (1975), p. 33-54.

Quasten, Johannes. *Patrology II*. Utrecht: Spectrum, 1953.

Säflund, Gösta. *De Pallio und die stilistische Entwicklung Tertullians*. Lund: CWK Gleerup, 1955.

Schmid, Ulrich. *Marcion und sein Apostolos*. Berlin: de Gruyter, 1995.

Schneemelcher, Wilhelm. "Bibel III". *Theologische Realenzyklopädie* 6 (1980), p. 22-48.

Schüle, Ernst Ulrich. "Der Ursprung des Bösen bei Marcion". *Zeitschrift für Religions- und Geistesgeschichte* 16 (1964), p. 23-42.

Soden, Hans von. "A. v. Harnacks Marcion". *Zeitschrift für Kirchengeschichte* 40 (1922), p. 191-206.

Stead, George Christopher. "In Search of Valentinus", in: Bentley Layton (ed.) *The Rediscovery of Gnosticism I*. Leiden: Brill, 1980, p. 75-102.

Stein, Arthur. *Der römische Ritterstand*. München: Beck, 1927.

Stewart-Sykes, Alistair. "Bread and fish, water and wine", in: Gerhard May/Katharina Greschat (ed.) *Marcion und seine kirchengeschichtliche Wirkung*. Berlin: de Gruyter, 2002, p. 207-220.

Stöckle, Albert. "Navicularii". *Paulys Real-Encyclopädie* 16 (1935), p. 1899-1932.

Tollinton, Richard Bartram. "The two elements in Marcion's dualism". *Journal of Theological Studies* 17 (1916), p. 263- 270.

1 These are signs of the membership of the *ordo equester*, cf. Arthur Stein, *Der römische Ritterstand*, München: Beck, 1927, p. 30-49. It is not certain that Marcion belonged to this social class. Peter Lampe, admitting that it is quite conceivable for a merchant from Asia Minor to be part of this class, doubts that Marcion would spend his money on social ascent, given his rigorous 'anti-world' asceticism (Peter Lampe, *Die stadtrömischen Christen in den ersten beiden Jahrhunderten*, Tübingen: Mohr, 1987, p. 208f.) However, although it is evident that Marcion would never use his money for personal vanities, it is not unlikely that he tried to benefit his cause by gaining an influential position in Roman society.

2 Apparently there was a general similarity between Marcionite and 'Catholic' rituals, cf. Adv. Marc. III.22,7 (hereafter all passages from Adv. Marc. are listed by number only).

3 In his work *De Pallio* Tertullian declares the *pallium*, unlike the toga, to be the appropriate clothing for Christians. Although this work dates from a later period of Tertullian's life, it does not necessarily follow that he did not wear the *pallium* until this time (against Gösta Säflund, *De Pallio und die stilistische Entwicklung Tertullians*, Lund: CWK Gleerup, 1955, p. 48).

4 It is most important to realize that Marcion was, although of course creator of his own doctrine too, not just a teacher (against Hubert Cancik, "Gnostiker in Rom. Zur Religionsgeschichte der Stadt Rom im 2. Jahrhundert nach Christus", in: Jacob Taubes (ed.), *Gnosis und Politik*, München: Wilhelm Fink, 1984, p. 176-178), but first of all a church founder and leader. Whether he was called 'bishop' during his lifetime we cannot certainly say, however, in Adamantius' Dialogue *De recta in Deum fide* the Marcionite Megethius states: "Marcion was my bishop" (I.8).

5 I,1,3.

6 The Roman poet Ovid was exiled to the city of Tomis at the Black Sea, in today's Romania. Here he wrote his *Tristia* and the *Epistulae ex Ponto*, in which he complains about the dreary life in Tomis, a city which he regarded as "the worst element in his cruel lot". Tertullian, however, does not refer to Ovid in his work.

7 I.1,3.

8 Sinope, Marcion's birthplace, the "Queen of the Pontus", was the earliest Greek colony (founded in the late seventh century BC) at the southern coast of the Black Sea, the "mother city of several small colonies" and an important commercial centre. It was therefore far from barbarous, cf. J. M. Cook, *The Greeks in Ionia and the East*, London: Thames and Hudson, 1962, p. 56f.

9 "Tertullian, a man well versed in the laws of the Romans" (Hist. eccl. II.2,4). I agree with Alexander Beck when he states: "Die Zuverlässigkeit dieser einzigen unmittelbaren und ältesten Überlieferung über die Juristenqualität Tertullians könnte nur beim Vorliegen ganz schwerwiegender Bedenken angezweifelt werden" (Alexander Beck, *Römisches Recht bei Tertullian und Cyprian*, Halle: Max Niemeyer, 1930, p. 39). Even if the identification of the Christian writer Tertullian with the Roman jurist of the same name is rather unlikely (cf. Timothy Barnes, *Tertullian: a historical and literary study*, Oxford: Clarendon Press, [2]1985, p. 22-29), I can see no conclusive reason to doubt the statement by Eusebius. Therefore I think it would be most fitting to apply the principle *in dubio pro reo* here and to sum up with Wolfgang Kunkel: "Bei dieser Sachlage entscheide ich mich dafür, daß wir von dem Juristen Tertullian nichts Verläßliches wissen, und verweise den Theologen in den Kreis der juristisch geschulten Rhetoren" (Wolfgang Kunkel, *Die römischen Juristen*, Köln: Böhlau, [2]2001, p. 240).

10 Pan. 42.1,5. Tertullian does not refer to this incident in his work against Marcion. He does not seem to know anything about Marcion's life before his arrival in Rome at all, and even states that Marcion came to Rome "primo calore fidei catholicae" (IV.4,3).

11 Pan. 42.1,4. The truthfulness of this statement about Marcion has been strongly doubted by modern scholars, who believe that this legend arose from Marcion's 'seduction of the church', cf. e.g. Morton Enslin, "The Pontic Mouse", *AThR* 27 (1945), p. 7: "The constant use of the figure 'virgin' for the church and the attempts at her 'defilement' by heretics is quite sufficient an explanation for the legend".

12   For this and the following, cf. *Prologus secundum Iohannem*, in: Jürgen Regul, *Die antimarcionitischen Evanglienprologe*, Freiburg: Herder, 1969, p. 34f.

13   It is quite likely that these "scripta vel epistolae [...] a fratibus qui in Ponto fuerunt" were indeed letters of recomendation, cf. Adolf von Harnack, *Marcion. Das Evangelium vom fremden Gott*, Darmstadt: Wissenschaftliche Buchgesellschaft, ²1996, p. 24. This demonstrates that Marcion's "excommunication at home had made some stir, and that he already had a following" (Enslin, *Mouse*, p. 7).

14   Marcion could be rejected or excommunicated several times since an excommunication was at that time limited to one community only, cf. Harnack, *Marcion*, p. 23f.

15   According to Pan. 42.1,7, Marcion arrived in Rome after the death of the Roman bishop Hyginus, i.e. about 140 AD.

16   Ep. 133,4: "Marcion Romam praemisit mulierem, quae decipiendos sibi animos praepararet." This information by Jerome is isolated and not very reliable.

17   "Er [Marcion] scheint mehrfach für kurze Zeit von der Gemeinschaft getrennt und dann wieder angenommen worden zu sein" (Lampe, *Christen*, p. 331).

18   The Marcionites posited 115 ½ years and six months between Christ (who appeared in the 15th year of Tiberius) and Marcion (I,19.2). This would bring us to the middle (ides?) of July 144, which can only be "das Jahr des vollendeten Bruches M.s mit der Kirche und der Gründung seiner eigenen Kirche" (Harnack, *Marcion*, p. 20*).

19   Praescr. 30 + IV.4,3.

20   V.1,2. The term "acatus" describes first of all a small und fast ship, but usually refers to pirate ships, cf. Karl Ernst Georges, *Ausführliches Lateinisch-Deutsches Handwörterbuch*, Vol. I, Darmstadt: Wissenschaftliche Buchgesellschaft, ⁸1998, p. 49. Given Tertullian's polemic style, it is more than likely that he intended this connotation.

21   Cf. Albert Stöckle, "Navicularii", *PRE* 16 (1935), p. 1911.

22 "It is not an exaggeration to say that the Church of Rome became very early the great laboratory of Christian and ecclesiastical policy" (George La Piana, "The Roman Church at the end of the second century", *HThR* 18 (1925), p. 203).

23 "Vielleicht hat auch die Erwägung Marcion zur Reise nach Rom bestimmt, daß dort der Bruch der Kirche mit dem Judentum vollständiger war als in Asien" (Harnack, *Marcion*, p. 25/n. 1). Furthermore, Lampe maintains that it might also have been business reasons which brought Marcion to Rome (Lampe, *Christen*, p. 206). Although this is possible, it seems fair to say that at this time of Marcion's life, missionary reasons were certainly more important to him.

24 We know little about the exact development of the Marcionite church. However, Justin (shortly after 150 AD) already states that Marcion's doctrine has spread "among all nations of the world" (Apol. I.26,5).

25 Walter Bauer considered the Roman character ("das Verständnis für Ordnung und Zucht, Gesetz und Regel") to be the decisive element in the successful fight against heresy (Walter Bauer, *Rechtgläubigkeit und Ketzerei im ältesten Christentum*, Tübingen: Mohr, [2]1964, p. 232).

26 Cf. Edwin C. Blackman, *Marcion and his Influence*, London: SPCK 1948, p. 10.

27 The role and the importance of Anicetus (?154-165) are highly disputed. He is sometimes referred to as the first 'pope', insofar as he is seen as the first representative of the monarchical episcopate in Rome, or at least as someone having an outstanding position within the Roman church, cf. Johannes Hofmann, "Die amtliche Stellung der in der ältesten römischen Bischofsliste überlieferten Männer in der Kirche von Rom", *HJ* 109 (1989). It is obvious that this is a classic point of controversy between catholic and protestant scholars. Thus, Lampe for example very much doubts the importance of Anicetus, cf. Lampe, *Christen*, 334-345.

28 It is improbable that Tertullian ever was in formal schism with the Catholic Church, cf. Douglas Powell, "Tertullianists and Cataphrygians", *VigChr* 29 (1975), p. 33-54.

29   Anicetus is considered both by Irenaeus (Adv. haer. III.3) and Hegesippus (Hist. eccl. IV.22,3) to be the rightful successor of the apostles.

30   Virg. I.3. This formula of the rule of faith is the freest of glosses and comments to be offered by Tertullian, cf. Johannes Quasten, *Patrology II*, Utrecht: Spectrum, 1953, p. 323.

31   We have no evidence of such a rule of faith used by Marcion or his followers. The one presented here is supposed to offer a short summary of Marcion's faith. It is deliberately formulated as a counterpart to Tertullian's rule, and mostly put together from Adv. haer. I.27,2 and IV.6,3.

32   I.1,6 + IV.4,1. This is the so-called "Präskriptionsbeweis", cf. E. P. Meijering, *Tertullian contra Marcion: Gotteslehre in der Polemik*, Leiden: Brill, 1977, p. 8-10.

33   Allegedly, Marcion made such a statement at the meeting with the church elders in 144 (Pan. 42.2,8). However, Harnack rightly remarked: "Diese dramatische Szene hat nichts Glaubwürdiges" (Harnack, *Marcion*, p. 27*).

34   Lk 6,43. Tertullian (I.2,1) describes this statement by Jesus as Marcion's "instinctus". Although it must be doubted that the parable was really the point of departure for Marcion's doctrine (cf. Barbara Aland, "Marcion", *TRE* 22 (1992), p. 93f.), a lot of church fathers mention this passage in context with Marcion – e.g. Origen, who even calls it the "quaestio famosissima" (Princ. II.5,4) – so that it must have had a great importance for him.

35   I.2,1.

36   I.13,2.

37   I.14,1.

38   I.13,5.

39   The evidence does, in my eyes, not support the idea of a metaphysical dualism between (evil) matter and (good) spirit in Marcion's thought, cf. Scene V. His pessimism of the world rather seems to originate from his negative view of man.

40 II.5,1.

41 II.5,1f.

42 Tertullian considers Marcion to be a follower of Epicurus (I.25,3), but he does interestingly not mention it in this context of thought, which was in fact typically Epicurean, cf. John Gager, "Marcion and Philosophy", *VigChr* 26 (1972), p. 55-58. From this similarity of thought Gager concludes that Marcion was indeed influenced by Epicurean philosophy. However, Lampe asked mockingly: "Schwingt sich nicht bereits ein Untersekundaner ohne den Steigbügel Epikurs zur selben Argumentation auf?", and describes the association of Marcion with pagan philosophers as "übliche Ketzerpolemik" (Lampe, *Christen*, p. 217f.) How arbitrary this association seems to have been becomes obvious when Tertullian calls Marcion elsewhere "Stoicae studiosus" (Praescr. 30.1). Tertullian's view that the philosophers are "haereticorum patriarchae" (Herm. 8.3) is also noteworthy.

43 II.5,1.

44 II.5,5.

45 II.2,7.

46 II.25,2.

47 II.7,2f.

48 Isa. 45.7. Tertullian refers to this statement (obviously one of the most important Old Testament passages for Marcion) several times in his work: e.g. I.2,2; II.14,1; II.24,4.

49 "He [Marcion] knew the Bible thoroughly and could quote texts in evidence with ready facility" (R. B. Tollinton, "The two elements in Marcion's dualism", *JThS* 17 (1916), p. 264f.).

50 II.14,2-4.

51 Ex. 20.5.

52 II.15,1

53 Jer. 31.29f.

54 II.15,2.

55 II.20,2f.

56 Jonah 3.10.

57 II.16,4.

58 II.16,5

59 II.16,6f.

60 II.24,8.

61 II.2,4. (Isa. 40.13).

62 As member of the equestrian order, Marcion would have been entitled to a special place in the theatre, cf. Stein, *Ritterstand*, p. 21-30.

63 "Summa offensa penes illum [Deum] idolatria est" (Spec. 2.9).

64 Although we have no immediate evidence of it (apart from the allusion in I.27,5), it is quite likely that Marcion rejected the theatre as well. The disapproval of the shows was common in early Christianity and Tertullian's position might be considered classical. However, given that the main reason for this rejection was that the theatre was seen as a "Hort unmoralischer Vergnügungen, die mit dem ethischen Anspuch des Christentums nicht vereinbar waren" (Ferdinand Barth ,"Theater", *TRE* 33 (2001), p. 178), I imagine Marcion to be capable of distinguishing between this kind of primitive pleasures and a great piece of art.

65 Spec. 2.11.

66 Deut. 22.5.

67 Spec. 23.5f.

68 These are Antigone's last words in Sophocles' play.

69 Spec. 15.4/6.

70 IV.6,3.

71 III.13,1 (Isa. 8,4).

72 III.13,2f.

73 III.13,3.

74 Marcion categorically rejected allegorical interpretation of (Old Testament) passages, cf. John Barton, "Marcion Revisited", in: Lee Martin McDonald/James A. Sanders (ed.), *The Canon debate*, Peabody: Hendrickson Publishers, 2002, p. 348-352.

75 III.13,3.

76 "Cellula creatoris" (I.14,2).

77 III.11,7.

78 Carn. IV.1.

79 III.8,1 (I. Joh. 4.2f.).

80 "Magister communis" (III.14,4).

81 V.20,3. (Ph. 2.7).

82 Lk 4.30.

83 IV.8,3.

84 III.8,5 (I. Cor. 15.3f.).

85 Marcion (probably) cut these words out of the epistle. For Marcion's technique of 'correcting' Scripture, cf. Scene IV.

86 A whole string of scholars – especially Harnack – has considered Marcion to be something like the "Martin Luther of the second century" (Enslin, *Mouse*, p. 6). Although certain similarities between the two cannot be overlooked, in the end Marcion turns out to have very little in common with the 16th century Reformer. First of all, Luther was a dialectical thinker, Marcion a radical dualist. For Luther it was Law *and* Gospel, for Marcion it was either or. Moreover, Luther had a completely different point of departure. It was his immense feeling of guilt which made him realize that he cannot reach justification before God by the works of the Law. As for Marcion, however, it was Hans von Soden who remarked most rightly "daß Marcion dem Schuldgedanken (und damit einem eigentlichen Sündenbewußtsein) völlig verschlossen ist" (Hans von Soden, "A. v. Harnacks Marcion", *ZKG* 40 (1922), p. 204).

87 Rec. I.27 (Gal. 3.13).

88 The high value Marcion attaches to the reality of Christ's death seems to be contradictory to his docetic view. However, Harnack stated correctly: "'Doketismus' bedeutete im antiken Zeitalter etwas anderes als heute, weil man die Konsequenzen nicht zog, die wir ziehen zu müssen glauben [...] Der Doketismus war in jener Zeit auch ein Ausdruck dafür, daß Christus nicht Produkt seiner Zeit ist und daß das Geniale und Göttliche sich nicht aus der Natur heraus entwickelt" (Harnack, *Marcion*, p. 125).

89 III.8,6.

90 This is Burkitt's translation of the words from the so-called *Proevangelium* of Marcion by an old Syrian (Anti-Marcionite) exegesis of the Lord's parables; quoted in: Joseph Hoffmann, *Marcion: on the Restitution of Christianity*, Chico: Scholars Press, 1984, p. 104. The English translation of the text in Hoffmann's book is useful, but his work cannot be safely used as a source for Marcion's thought, as Gerhard May has shown in his devastating, though correct review (Gerhard May, "Ein neues Markionbild?", *ThR* 51 (1986), p. 404-413).

91 I.19,1. Marcion's God has been revealed "per semetipsum". For the question of a modalistic Christology in Marcion's thought, cf. Aland, *Marcion*, p. 96f.

92 III.8,1.

93 I.10,1.

94 I.2,3. The term "lippientibus" actually just refers to a sickness of the eyes, however, given the remark on double-vision, I think it is safe to assume that the meaning implied must be drunkenness.

95 For the usage of this term which is "isolée dans la latinité", cf. René Braun, *Deus Christianorum*, Paris: Etudes Augustiniennes, [2]1977, p. 43f.

96 I.3,2-5.

97 I.3,1. The "veritas Christiana" probably refers to the rule of faith, cf. Meijering, *Tertullian*, p. 14.

98 I have already tried to show that it is most unlikely that Marcion was immediately influenced by a certain philosophical school, cf. Scene

II, n. 42. However, Marcion's opinion about philosophy in general is not easy to determine. Harnack believes that Marcion completely rejected philosophy as "leeren Betrug" (Harnack, *Marcion*, p. 93), Lampe more or less concurs (Lampe, *Christen*, p. 216) and also Enrico Norelli describes Marcion's method as "bewußt antiphilosophisch" (Enrico Norelli, "Marcion: ein christlicher Philosoph oder ein Christ gegen die Philosophie?", in: Gerhard May, Katharina Greschat (ed.), *Marcion und seine kirchengeschichtliche Wirkung*, Berlin: de Gruyter, 2002, p. 128.) Even if Marcion's view on philosophy may not have been quite as negative as these scholars assume, I think it is fair to say that Tertullian's philosophical argumentation would have been in no way appealing, much less convincing to Marcion (cf. Blackman, *Marcion*, p. 71).

99 The nature or rather the source of Marcion's dualism (and thus of his whole theology) is highly disputed. Traditionally we can detect two opposing lines of interpretation. Some scholars consider Marcion's dualism to be derived from the oriental opposition of two cosmic principles (e.g. Wilhelm Bousset, *Hauptprobleme der Gnosis*, Göttingen: Vandenhoeck & Ruprecht, 1907, p. 109-113). Others prefer the option that Marcion was a real Biblicist, who found his dualism in Scripture (e.g. Eugène de Faye. *Gnostiques et gnosticisme*, Paris: Geuthner, [2]1925, p. 156-160). I believe that the second attempt of explanation is closer to the truth. The real issue for Marcion was his conviction that the Gospel was irreconcilable with the 'Old Testament'. However, the fact that he did not simply reject the 'Old Testament' (which is more or less Harnack's solution) but believed it to be the revelation of another God, who is the Creator, makes it clear that there must have been certain dualistic premises on his part, combined with a distinctive pessimism of the world (cf. Scene II, n. 39).

100 I.8,1.

101 I.8,2.

102 Cf. Scene I.

103 IV.25,10 (Lk 10.22).

104 I.13,3.

105 I.17,1.

106 Cf. Rec. 2.4. Cf. also the relevant passages in Romans (1.16, 10.4).

107 I.23,3.

108 I.22,4.

109 It is uncertain, however likely, that Christ's descent into Hades was already part of the Church tradition in Marcion's time; cf. Ernst Koch, "Höllenfahrt Christi", *TRE* 15 (1986), p. 456f.

110 Adv. haer. I.27,3.

111 Jerome describes Marcion as "doctissimus" (Comm. Os. II.10,1).

112 "Marcion did not, as is commonly said, reject the OT. He took it literally, and as divine revelation" (Stuart G. Hall, "Marcion", *A Dictionary of Biblical Interpretation*, London: SCM Press, 1990, p. 423).

113 "Proprius deus Iudaicae gentis" (IV.33,4).

114 IV.6,1.

115 IV.1,1.

116 In this context, I deliberately avoided mentioning the alleged (yet most famous) antithesis of Marcion between the *just* and the *good* God (cf. Harnack, *Marcion*, p. 262*-264*). This idea is, in my eyes, nothing else but another anachronistic projection of Reformation theology onto Marcion (cf. Winrich Löhr, "Did Marcion distinguish between a just and a good God?", in: Gerhard May (ed.), *Marcion*, p. 131-146).

117 II.21,2 (Num 15.32-36).

118 IV.12,3.

119 IV.12,5 (Lk 6.1-5). As to the content of Marcion's 'Bible', I rely first of all on Harnack (*Marcion*, p. 67*-127* and p. 183*-240*), and also on Ulrich Schmid (*Marcion und sein Apostolos*, Berlin: de Gruyter, 1995, p. I/315-I344). That these reconstructions can only be approximate is evident.

120 IV.12,10. (Ex 12.16).

121 IV.12,14. (Matt 5.17).

122 V.14,6 (Rom 10.4).

123 IV.2,3.

124 IV.2,1f.

125 IV.2,2.

126 V.2,4 (Gal. 1.6f.).

127 "Warum Markion sein vermeintliches Urevangelium gerade hinter dem Lukasevangelium zu entdecken meinte, läßt sich nicht mehr sicher ausmachen [...] Lukas bot alles in allem die geringsten Schwierigkeiten" (Hans Freiherr von Campenhausen, *Die Entstehung der christlichen Bibel*, Tübingen: Mohr, 1968, p. 187f.).

128 I.20,4 (Gal 2.4). Paul's letter to the Galatians was obviously Marcion's main source for his conspiracy theory and provided him with sufficient justification for his process of 'cleaning': "Er [Marcion] las dann die ersten beiden Kapitel des Galaterbriefes gleichsam als historische Einleitung in das Briefcorpus. Es lag nahe, das gesamte Denken und Wirken des Apostels im Lichte dieser Darlegungen zu verstehen." (Gerhard May, "Der Streit zwischen Petrus und Paulus in Antiochien bei Markion", in: Walter Homolka/Otto Ziegelmeier (ed.), *Von Wittenberg nach Memphis. Festschrift für Reinhard Schwarz*, Göttingen: Vandenhoeck & Ruprecht, 1989, p. 209).

129 IV.6,2.

130 V.3,2.

131 I.20,1.

132 V.1,2.

133 I.20,2. (Gal 2.14).

134 V.2,1.

135 V.2,4 + V.3,7.

136 IV.11,9 (Isa. 43.19).

137 Marcion sometimes also added or changed words, however, "die Streichungen sind ja doch die Hauptsache in seinem Verfahren" (Harnack, *Marcion*, p. 70).

138 Marcion included all letters attributed to Paul into his 'Bible', except the Pastoral Epistles, probably because they had simply never come into his view (cf. ibid., p. 170*f.).

139 "Idee und Wirklichkeit einer christlichen Bibel sind von Marcion geschaffen worden, und die Kirche, die sein Werk verwarf, ist ihm hierin nicht vorangegangen, sondern – formal gesehen – seinem Vorbild nachgefolgt" (Campenhausen, *Entstehung*, p. 174) Even if Marcion's large influence on the development of the Christian Bible might be doubted (cf. Wilhelm Schneemelcher, "Bibel III", *TRE* 6 (1980), p. 36-38), it is widely agreed that Marcion was the first to have a closed canon of Christian writings (cf. John Knox, *Marcion and the New Testament*, Chicago: University of Chicago Press, 1942, p. 19-38).

140 It was Wolfram Kinzig who proposed that Marcion was the first to give the title 'New Testament' to a canonical collection of texts, in opposition to the outdated 'Old Testament' of the Jews (Wolfram Kinzig, "Kaine Diatheke: The Title of the New Testament in the second and third Centuries", *JThS* 45 (1994), p. 541-544). Although we cannot be absolutely sure who actually invented the terms 'Old' and 'New Testament', who would be more likely to have done so than the undisputed master of Antitheses, the most forceful advocate of the utter newness of the Gospel?

141 IV.6,2.

142 Cf. Harnack, *Marcion*, p. 42f.

143 I.1,5.

144 The personal relation between Marcion and Ptolemaeus is hard to judge. "Ist der christliche römische Lehrer Ptolemäus, den Justin in der sog. zweiten Apologie erwähnt, mit dem bekannten römischen Valentinianer gleichen Namens identisch (was nicht unwahrscheinlich), so kann sich M. mit diesem in Rom berührt haben" (Harnack, *Marcion*, p. 29f.). The relation between Marcion and the Gnostics in general, however, is even harder to judge and represents one of the most disputed questions among scholars. Harnack's classic view that Marcion has to be seen in sharp (although not complete) distinction from the Gnostics has been widely contested in subsequent scholarship. Ugo Bianchi concludes: "Marcion [...] appartient de plein droit à l'histoire du gnosticisme. Il y appartient, c'est vrai, de façon originale, sur la base d'un certain radicalisme qui s'inspire des lignes simples décrites par Harnack, mais qui se nourrit de l'*humus* riche et polyvalent du dualisme de la gnose classique" (Ugo Bianchi, "Marcion: Theologien Biblique ou Docteur Gnostique?", *VC* 21 (1967), p. 149). Christoph Markschies, however, recently expressed the most interesting theory that it was not Marcion who was influenced by the Gnosis, but that in fact Gnostics such as Ptolemaeus reacted to *his* system: "Mindestens die valentinianische Gnosis und die Entwicklung ihrer Systeme können ein gutes Stück weit als gegen Marcion gerichtetes Konzept begriffen werden" (Christoph Markschies, "Die valentianische Gnosis und Marcion – einige neue Perspektiven", in: Gerhard May (ed.), *Marcion*, p. 174).

145 "Niemand kann die uns erhaltenen Fragmente des Valentin lesen, ohne sich von dem hohen Geiste und der feinen Bildung dieses Mannes berührt zu fühlen. Dasselbe gilt von seinen Schülern Ptolemäus und Herakleon" (Harnack, *Mission und Ausbreitung des Christentums*, Leipzig: Hinrich, 1902, p. 378). That Ptolemaeus and other Gnostic leaders were highly intelligent and educated people, is undisputed. Lampe, however, although concurring that the Gnostic teachers were intellectuals, tried to show "dass der valentinianische Anhang dieser Lehrer halb- und ungebildet sein kann" (Lampe, *Christen*, p. 257).

146 Irenaeus (Adv. haer. I.13,3) reports that the Valentinian Marcus busies himself especially with "mulieres ditissimae".

147 Praescr. 38.7-10. Tertullian here compares Marcion's and Valentinus' attitude towards Scripture, concluding that Valentinus was, although of course not correct in his interpretation of Scripture, not as bad as Marcion was. As to the relation between Valentinus and the 'Valentinians' (such as Ptolemaeus), George C. Stead critically remarked that "there is a sharp contrast between the fragments from his [Valentinus'] own writings preserved by Clement and the complex cosmic myth known from the heresiologists' account of the Valentinians" (G. C. Stead, "In Search of Valentinus", in: Bentley Layton (ed.), *The Rediscovery of Gnosticism I*, Leiden: Brill, 1980, p. 95). Be that as it may, this statement refers to the elaborate mythological system

of Ptolemaeus and not so much to his exegesis. Thus it seems quite possible that in this matter Ptolemaeus was not so different from his 'master', given that Valentinus is also said to add "dispositiones non comparentium rerum" (Praescr. 38.10) to the Scriptures.

148 The description of Ptolemaeus's system in this scene is based on Adv. haer. I.1-8. For a good survey of the system, cf. Bentley Layton (ed. and tr.), *The Gnostic Scriptures*, New York: Doubleday, 1987, p. 276-280.

149 Adv. haer. I.1,3.

150 Valentinus's Fragment 4, in: Markschies, *Valentinus Gnosticus?*, Tübingen: Mohr, 1992, p. 118.

151 The relation between Valentinus and Ptolemaeus is uncertain (see already above n. 147). Markschies sums up: "Wir wissen nicht, in welchem Verhältnis die beiden zueinander standen" (ibid., p. 393). However, even if Ptolemaeus advanced and thereby changed Valentinus' original teaching, I think it is safe to assume that he was indeed a follower of his.

152 For the Gnostic idea of a 'call', cf. Werner Foerster, "Die Grundzüge der Ptolemäischen Gnosis", *NTS* 6 (1960), p. 28f.

153 This is a distinctive difference within the doctrine of Ptolemaeus compared to Marcion's: "Le premier Dieu n'est pas totalement séparé du monde d'ici-bas (comme il l'est dans la doctrine de Marcion), mais, au contraire, toutes choses dépendent de lui [Pan. 33.7,6]" (Winrich A. Löhr, "La doctrine de Dieu dans la lettre a Flora de Ptolémée", *RHPR* 75 (1995), p. 186).

154 Pan. 33.7,5-7.

155 Aland considers this anthropological view to be the main difference between Marcion and the Gnostics, cf. Barbara Aland, "Marcion: Versuch einer neuen Interpretation", *ZThK* 70 (1973), p. 433-435.

156 The relation between Cerdo and Marcion is – once again – uncertain: "That there was a Gnostic in the second century named Cerdo who may have met or associated with Marcion seems possible. That this Cerdo actually taught the exact 'identical' teachings that Marcion

taught, as presented by the Fathers, is obviously a projection and is highly suspect" (David Deakle, "Harnack & Cerdo", in: Gerhard May (ed.), *Marcion*, p. 190).

157 Pan. 33.3,5. Ptolemaeus' reference to this position about the Law in his letter to Flora is probably directed against Marcion, although it is obviously distorted; cf. Winrich Löhr, "Die Auslegung des Gesetzes bei Markion, den Gnostikern und den Manichäern", in: Georg Schöllgen/ Clemens Scholten (ed.), *Stimuli. Exegese und ihre Hermeneutik in Antike und Christentum. Festschrift für Ernst Dassmann*, Münster: Aschendorff, 1996, p. 80/n. 11.

158 "Für Ptolemäus sind – wie für Markion – der Schöpfer dieser Welt und der Gesetzgeber identisch" (ibid., p. 83).

159 According to Epiphanius (Pan. 42.3,3) Marcion used water in the sacraments, which makes it quite likely – given his rigorous asceticism in general – that he was a strict teetotaller (against Alistair Stewart-Sykes, "Bread and fish, water and wine", in: May (ed.), *Marcion*, p. 212-214).

160 I.14,4. Marcion's vegetarianism (Ref. 7.30,3f.) is probably just an ascetic action. This would explain why he did eat fish which is "seen in the ancient world as a simple and ascetic food" (ibid., p. 215).

161 V.13,13f. (Rom 7.12).

162 V.13,15.

163 I.27,1.

164 Comm. Rom. V.6,2 (Rom. 5.20).

165 V.8,3.

166 II.5,7.

167 I.27,2f.

168 I.27,4.

169 I.27,5.

170 The classic view that Tertullian's theology is based on the ideas of *satisfactio* and *meritum* has been impressively refuted by Gösta Hallonsten (*Satisfactio bei Tertullian*, Malmö: CWK Gleerup, 1984;

idem, *Meritum bei Tertullian*, Malmö: CWK Gleerup, 1985).

171 II.13,5.

172 Ux. I.2,2.

173 "Tertullien a beaucoup écrit sur le mariage, et sur aucun sujet il ne s'est tant contredit" (Adhémar d'Alès, *La théologie de Tertullien*, Paris: Beauchesne, [2]1905, p. 370). Tertullian's opinions on marriage and chastity are indeed not always consistent throughout his works, to say the least. The following statements are therefore exclusively based on his view in *Adversus Marcionem*.

174 I.29,2.

175 I.29,7.

176 IV.9,3. The term "companions in misery" is probably a self-designation of the Marcionites (cf. Aland, *Marcion*, p. 97).

177 III.24,1.

178 I.27,6. Marcion's statements on eschatology (as portrayed by Tertullian) are full of inconsistencies, cf. Harnack, *Marcion. Der moderne Gläubige des 2. Jahrhunderts, der erste Reformator*, edited by Friedemann Steck, Berlin: de Gruyter, 2003, p. 266-270. Although inconsistencies within a system are not uncommon, it seems more likely to me that Tertullian was not able or not willing to understand Marcion's conception correctly, or that he even distorted Marcion's eschatology deliberately. I shall therefore only broach the topic in this scene.

179 I.28,1.

180 Polycarp came to Rome in the time of Anicetus (Hist. eccl. V.24,16), who was probably responsible for the "Außenkontakte der stadtröm. Gemeinde" (Lampe, "Anicetus", *RGG* 1 (1998), p. 503).

181 Hist. eccl. V.20,6.

182 Hist. eccl. IV.14,5/V.24,16f.

183 Adv. haer. III.3,4.

184 "Die Organisation, der Kultus, die Schrift, sie alle behalten in der heranwachsenden Kirche Marcion's ihre alte Gültigkeit. Aber eben dies war es, was die Apologeten der Großkirche so in Harnisch brachte und in Marcion den gefährlichen Erzketzer sehen ließ" (Ernst Ulrich Schüle, "Der Ursprung des Bösen bei Marcion", ZRGG 16 (1964), p. 29).

185 Ezek. Hom. 7.3.

186 Ernst Barnikol (*Die Entstehung der Kirche im zweiten Jahrhundert und die Zeit Marcions*, 1933) considered the meeting between Anicetus and Polycarp to be the "birth-hour" of the Catholic Church. Blackman summarizes: "The importance of that meeting for Barnikol lies not in the discussion about Fasting or the Eucharist, but in the probability that the two bishops then made a common front against Marcion" (Blackman, *Marcion*, p. 21). However, Blackman also remarked correctly that this proposition is "highly suggestive".

187 Lk 5.37. Allegedly, Marcion asked the elders to interpret this statement at the assembly which rejected him in 144 (Pan. 42.2,1).

188 Pan. 42.2,3.

189 IV.11,9

190 Adv. haer. III.3,4. It is quite possible that the meeting described by Irenaeus between Polycarp and Marcion did indeed happen during Polycarp's visit to Rome.

191 Hom. Luc. 25.5

192 The fact that the members of Marcion's church did not procreate was probably one major reason for its decline (cf. Harnack, *Marcion*, p. 148f.).